DIGITAL AND INFORMATION LITERACY ™

DESIGNING, BUILDING, AND MAINTAINING WEB SITES

J. POOLOS

rosen publishing's
rosen
central®

New York

*This book is dedicated to all of the hardworking people
who make the Internet happen.*

Published in 2011 by The Rosen Publishing Group, Inc.
29 East 21st Street, New York, NY 10010

Library of Congress Cataloging-in-Publication Data

Poolos, Jamie.
Designing, building, and maintaining web sites / J. Poolos. — 1st ed.
    p. cm. — (Digital and information literacy)
Includes bibliographical references and index.
ISBN 978-1-4358-9424-2 (library binding)
ISBN 978-1-4488-0594-5 (pbk)
ISBN 978-1-4488-0607-2 (6-pack)
1. Web site development—Juvenile literature. 2. Web sites—Design—Juvenile literature.
I. Title.
TK5105.888.P585 2011
006.7—dc22

                                                                        2010003052

Manufactured in the United States of America

CPSIA Compliance Information: Batch #S10YA: For further information, contact Rosen Publishing, New York, New York, at 1-800-237-9932.

CONTENTS

INTRODUCTION

Today, virtually anyone who has access to an Internet connection can create a Web site. There are many different kinds of Web sites, but they all work more or less the same way. A Web site is a collection of pages on the World Wide Web. Web sites are usually devoted to a single topic, such as the Revolutionary War, or provide a service, such as delivering the news. The Web pages that make a Web site are linked together with hyperlinks.

People who create Web sites, known as Web developers, must make a number of important decisions when planning a site. These decisions affect the three phases of developing a Web site: designing the site, building it, and publishing it.

Each phase of Web site planning requires different kinds of skills. For example, in order to make a Web site look good and appeal to a visitor, the person designing the site must understand the principles of graphic design and how pictures, headings, text, and colors can work together on a Web page to make it more visually appealing. In order to make the Web site reliable and fast, the person writing the code for the site has to know what programming languages to use to construct the site. It is also useful for people who have built a Web site to understand how the site works when a

visitor interacts with it. This knowledge can come in handy when it's necessary to identify and fix problems that occur with the site.

It doesn't take years and years of training to design and build a Web site. A young person can create a Web site from scratch by knowing the basics of the how Web sites work and the steps required to plan, design, build, publish, and maintain them. The process of creating a Web site can teach anyone a number of useful computer and problem-solving skills. When a person creates a Web site, he or she is joining a club of hundreds of thousands of other young people who have done the same.

Chapter 1

How a Web Site Works

Web site is made of code that is delivered to a user by his or her computer. When a user clicks on a Web link, he or she is actually asking the computer to deliver another Web page. The computer registers the request and delivers the page. If there is a problem delivering the page, the computer sends a message to the user.

Web sites operate on the World Wide Web. In the most basic sense, the Web is a network of computers all over the world. These computers all communicate with one another on the Internet, allowing billions of people to be connected online.

People use Web sites to share information and exchange text, pictures, videos, audio, and software applications. News agencies like CNN, the *Wall Street Journal*, and the *New York Times* publish news stories and videos online. Universities offer classes online, so students can learn from home. Stores of all kinds sell their products over the Internet. Individuals publish their ideas on blogs.

People all over the world use the Internet. Here, students learn about new technologies and advancements in the World Wide Web at the 7th Internet Festival in Abidjan, Ivory Coast.

Although billions of people all over the world use the Web for these and other purposes, it wasn't all that long ago that the Internet didn't even exist. In fact, up until the 1960s, the idea of sharing information between computers was just a dream. At this time, the U.S. Department of Defense began work on creating a network of computers. In 1985, an American research organization called the National Science Foundation developed what we now know as the Internet.

File   Edit   View   Favorites   Tools   Help

THE FAST-PACED WORLD OF THE WEB

The Fast-Paced World of the Web

As new technologies are developed to satisfy the needs of consumers, old technologies fade away. Most say current Web technology becomes out of date within three years' time. The rapid forward march of technology brings new capabilities to the Web every day.

Improving data transfer rates are one of the main forces driving change on the Web. Up until recently, the gold standard for data transfer was a T-1 line that could transfer up to 1.5 megabytes per second. Now the Internet can achieve five times that. Because data can now be exchanged at a much higher rate, Web developers can include rich animation and videos in their Web sites.

As the Internet developed and became easier to use, people immediately saw its potential. Large communications organizations, such as phone companies, built their own networks. Soon, there were many networks connected to one another. It was then that an Englishman named Tim Berners-Lee began to experiment with the concept of linking one piece of information to another over a network. In 1991, the World Wide Web became available to the public. Now people could easily share information, no matter where they lived or worked.

Web Pages, Web Browsers, and Web Servers

The Internet is a network of computers that resembles a series of paths over which data travels. The Web is an application, or program, that runs on the

Internet. It's a series of documents and other kinds of information that are connected by hyperlinks. The three components that make this happen are the Web page, the Web browser, and the Web server.

A Web browser is a software application used to retrieve Web pages from Web servers and to present them in a form a user can read. Web browser applications are installed on a user's personal computer, called a client. Some popular browsers include Internet Explorer, Mozilla Firefox, and Safari. Web browsers display HTML documents. HTML stands for hypertext markup language. Composed of text, HTML documents include both content and directions that tell the browser how to display the content. For example, a Web page may display the word "Hello." The HTML document contains this content (the word "Hello") and guidelines for its display—such as centered on the page and in 12-point type.

A Web server is a computer program that delivers (or serves) Web pages when someone requests them. The term "server" can also refer to the computers on which Web server software runs. Servers are not like the personal computers people use in their day-to-day lives. Instead, they are generally large machines that are kept in special climate-controlled rooms.

Web pages, browsers, and servers all work together over the Internet to make communication possible. This is how the process works:

1. A student sitting at a computer connected to the Internet opens a Web browser, types http://www.nasa.gov into the browser address field, and presses the return key.
2. The Web browser connects to the server where the NASA home page is stored and requests the page.
3. The server sends the page back to the student's Web browser. The page is sent as HTML text.
4. The Web browser reads the HTML, deciphers it, formats the information (including text, pictures, and video), and then displays it on the screen as a Web page that the student can read.

Successful Web sites are the result of thorough, well thought-out designs. Web designers must take great care to plot the flow of the Web site so users can easily navigate from one page to another.

Breaking the Code: HTML

Before the Web page can be stored on a server and served to the student's computer, someone has to create it. Web pages contain directions that tell the browser how to display the content. Those directions are contained in HTML tags.

When a person creates a Web page in a text editor or an HTML editor, he or she places the HTML code in brackets, called tags. HTML tags tell the Web browser a number of things, like to display text in a particular color and size. HTML tags also tell the browser to set the text in a certain number of columns, or to place a picture in the middle of the page. Here's an example of HTML:

This text is bold.

A Web page is constructed of code that contains both the content displayed on the page (or references to files containing the content) and directions that tell the browser how to display the content.

The "b" within the tags tells the browser to make the text between the tags bold. When displayed on a Web page, the sentence would look like this:

This text is **bold**.

The tags don't display on the Web page. Only the sentence displays, along with the formatting—in this case, the bold typeface.

HTML is the building block for Web page authoring, but there are other programming languages that can tell the browser how to display a Web page. These include CSS, Flash, JavaScript, and XML. These languages are more sophisticated and powerful than HTML, and they allow knowledgeable Web page authors to build fast, user-friendly Web sites.

Chapter 2

Planning a Web Site

One of the most important tasks a person creating a Web site must undertake is planning the site. A well-defined plan serves as a roadmap for the entire project. Without a plan, a person developing a Web site won't know the most efficient way to create the site. Instead, he or she will waste a lot of time and do a lot of unnecessary work while coming up with a good design. Planning things out first makes designing and building a Web site faster and easier.

Defining the Purpose of the Web Site

The first thing to do when developing a plan is to determine what the goal of the site is. Every Web site begins with a goal of what a Web developer hopes to achieve. The goal will determine the direction that the Web design takes. One way to determine the goal of a Web site is to define its purpose. It's best to start with as broad an idea as possible, and then narrow it down.

For example, the goal of a Web site could be to deliver information about horses to people, or to sell books about veterinary medicine, or to allow people

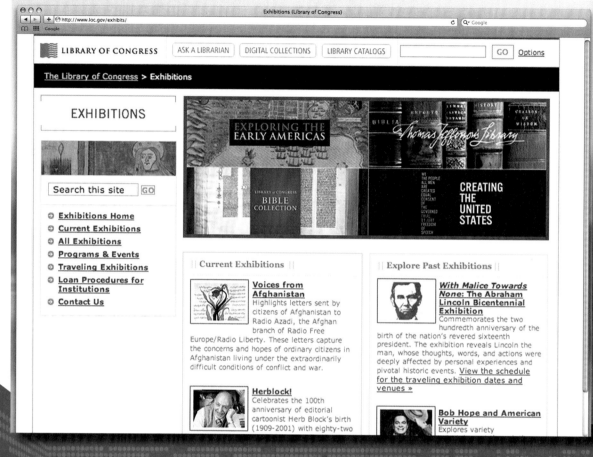

The home page of the Web site of the Library of Congress displays in a clean, user-friendly, three-column design. The large graphic near the top cycles through a series of images, each of which links to a feature.

who are interested in becoming veterinarians to talk on the Web. Once the goal of the site is established, it is easier to determine how to best achieve it.

The next step is to determine the objective. That is, how will the goal be best achieved? If the goal is to deliver information about horses, the first thing to consider is exactly what kind of information about horses will be communicated by the Web site. If the site is simply going to provide information and nothing else, it will probably include pictures, text, and maybe videos. If the site is going to sell books, it should be designed as an online store. The person designing the site would want it to display the books so potential buyers could view them. The site might also describe the books in detail, show their price, allow customers to buy books with their credit cards, and provide them with a way to check on their orders.

It's important to match the Web site's objectives to its goal. Any objective that doesn't meet a need of the goal should be discarded.

Defining the Target Audience

After the Web site designer has determined the Web site's basic needs, it's time to consider the needs of the site's audience. These are the people who the designer believes will want to visit the Web site. Everyone in the audience will have something in common. For example, every member of an audience that visits a Web site discussing different kinds of horse-riding competitions will have a general interest in horses.

Defining a site's audience allows the person designing it to eliminate people who have no interest in the site's topic. The developer can then focus the site's content on what will appeal to its target audience.

_ □ X

File   Edit   View   Favorites   Tools   Help

WEB ANALYTICS

Web Analytics

Web analytics programs gather and analyze Web usage data. Web analytics measure Web site traffic and serve as the basis for user analyses. There are two ways data is gathered. One is by log file analysis, in which the Web server's transactions are counted and analyzed. The second is by tagging, which records the number of times a Web page is rendered. Together, these measures help individuals and businesses make decisions about their Web sites.

Doing research is the best way to determine who the target audience is. The Internet can provide a number of clues about the general target audience of a Web site. For example, a person creating a Web site about the Revolutionary War might run a search to identify other sites that discuss the topic. He or she might talk to classmates and teachers about their interest in the Revolutionary War and determine what they might want to see in a site on the topic. He or she can learn more about the subject by talking to an expert about the Revolutionary War to find out what kind of information people are looking for.

Developing Content

Once the target audience has been identified, the next step is to consider what would appeal to it. Will people visiting the Web site already have a

Web designers often work in teams. Compromise is a major part of the design process and part of the challenge. Here, a user interface designer and a programmer discuss ways to improve the user experience of a prototype Web site.

basic knowledge of the subject the site covers, or will they need a thorough explanation of the basics? It's important to match the content to the target audience's knowledge level.

At this point, the exact information that the Web site needs to contain should be identified. To accomplish this, it can be helpful to make a list of all of the topics or items of information the Web site will cover. (At this stage in the creation of the Web site, it's not necessary to organize these topics and items. That comes later.) The amount of detail the Web site will contain must be decided as well. Although more detail usually means more work, an audience will get a lot more out of a detailed Web site.

Once the site's content has been determined, it's time to decide how best to deliver the information to the audience. There are many options for presenting content on the Web. Each serves a specific purpose, and each has a cost.

Media	Use	Cost
TEXT	Text can be used to present complex information or provide quick verbal explanations.	Text can take up a lot of space. On its own, text is not very flashy.
PHOTOGRAPHS	Images enhance a story and can provide information at a glance.	Photographs can be hard to get. In addition, some time is required to manage image files. Too many image files can slow down the Web site.
ILLUSTRATIONS	Much like photographs, illustrations can enhance a story and provide information at a glance. They can also give the site character.	Creating illustrations can be time consuming. Illustrations also have the same issues as photographs when it comes to slowing down a Web site.
VIDEO	Video can tell a story and show real action in a way text can't.	Video can take time to create, process, and load to the Web server. Videos can also slow down the Web site.

After defining the target audience, creating the content the audience wants or needs, and determining how to deliver the content, it's time to begin the process of organizing the content into Web pages and designing the actual Web site.

Chapter 3

Designing a Web Site

A Web site designer focuses on three areas of design: the structure of the entire Web site, the layout of the Web pages, and Web site navigation. The goal is to organize the Web site in such a way that the visitor can easily navigate the site and find the information he or she wants. It is also important to design the Web pages so that they are easy to read.

Web Site Structure

Web site structure is important for two reasons. The first reason is that people who use a Web site want to be able to get to the content without a lot of fuss. They don't want to get lost on the site or wonder if they should click one link or another to find the information they want. The second reason is that search engine spiders—automated programs that gather information on Web sites and give it to search engines—do a better job if the site is easy to navigate.

The simplest way to think about Web site structure is to imagine levels, called tiers. A Web site is best organized in three tiers. The home page is tier 1. It is the page where visitors land when they type the Web site's URL into their browsers. Think of it as a gateway to the Web site. The tier 2 pages include most of the broad-level content. Each of these pages may link to any number of tier 3 pages, which include more detailed information.

At this point in the design process, most Web developers create site map diagrams to show the organization of their Web sites. A site map diagram is a simple illustration describing a Web site's structure:

TIER 1	**Home Page**				
TIER 2	About Horses	Caring for Horses	How to Buy a Horse	Horse Gallery	My Horse Blog
TIER 3	Equine History Work Horses Recreational Horses Sports	Daily Care Veterinary Care		Gallery One Gallery Two	

Notice that three of the five tier 2 pages link to tier 3 pages, while "How to Buy a Horse" and "My Horse Blog" do not link to tier 3 pages. This is because these categories do not contain enough content to justify tier 3 pages. By employing the tiered system of Web site structure, Web site designers can build sites that are easy to use.

Web Page Elements

Not only is it important to create a solid Web site structure for ease of use, it's vital to make Web pages easy to read, attractive, and fast. Accomplishing this is all about arranging the content. Most Web pages are constructed with a few common elements. Some of these include:

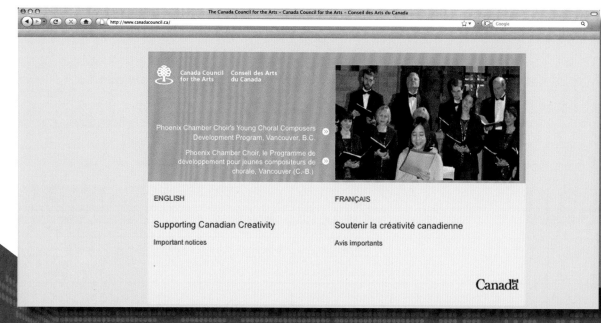

Some multilanguage Web sites use a home page as a language filter. When a user selects a language at the Web site of the Canada Council for the Arts (http://www.canadacouncil.ca), the landing page and all subsequent pages display in that language.

Background: The background of a Web page is what displays behind the text. It can be a plain colored field, a pattern, or a photograph.

Banners: Banners sit at the top of the page and usually show the Web site name. They may include illustrations or images.

Fonts: A font is a specific style and size of type within a type family. The fonts Ariel and Helvetica work best on most Web browsers.

Footer: The footer is like the banner, but it appears at the bottom of the page. It usually contains copyright information or contact information.

Headings: Headings are titles that separate one text block from another. They usually display in a darker and larger typeface than the regular body text.

Images: Images can be used to communicate ideas and add color to a page. They are most effective when they are used intelligently with text.

The landing page of the Web site of NASA (http://www.nasa.gov) utilizes multiple navigation menus, reflecting a design philosophy that minimizes blind exploration and helps users easily choose from the site's main content areas without having to visit intermediate pages.

Navigation menu: The navigation menu includes the links to other pages on the Web site. It usually appears across the top of the page, under the banner, or along the left side of the page.

Text blocks: Text blocks can be one or more paragraphs of words on the page. Text can display in many different colors. A page may include multiple text blocks.

Designing Web Pages

All of these elements are usually arranged in columns on the page. (A column is a division of a page from top to bottom.) The most popular layouts use two or three columns. Most pages of a Web site will have an identical layout. Some pages may require a different design. For instance, a typical information page may use three columns, while a gallery of photographs may use only two columns.

| File | Edit | View | Favorites | Tools | Help |

THE BLOG PHENOMENON

The Blog Phenomenon

According to cyberjournalist.net, on July 31, 2006, a Web site called Technorati tracked its fifty millionth blog. By 2009, there were more than two hundred million blogs worldwide. Easy to create, manage, and update, blogs are personal Web sites that allow individuals and organizations to share information quickly and easily. Blogs are used by journalists, political campaign managers, and experts of all kinds. They have become an important source of news and information for many users of the Web.

It's important to keep a Web site's goal, target audience, and content in mind when designing the layout. Web pages with muted colors and uncluttered layouts are often more appealing and easier to read and use than confusing pages with bright colors.

When using images on a Web site, consider how many images will be loaded as well as their size. Images are loaded from the Web server and display in the browser, just like text. Anyone designing a site should be careful not to use too many images on each page. This is because images take longer to load from the Web server than text does. Once an image is loaded, it is stored in the browser's cache. An image can be loaded from the cache more quickly than it can be loaded from the server. Web developers take advantage of this and try to use the same image on several Web pages in order to reduce loading time.

Acceptable image formats for use in a Web site include GIF (graphics interchange format) and JPEG (Joint Photographic Experts Group format). GIF files are best for line-art illustrations, like drawings. JPEG files are best for photographs. If an image is in some other format, it must be converted

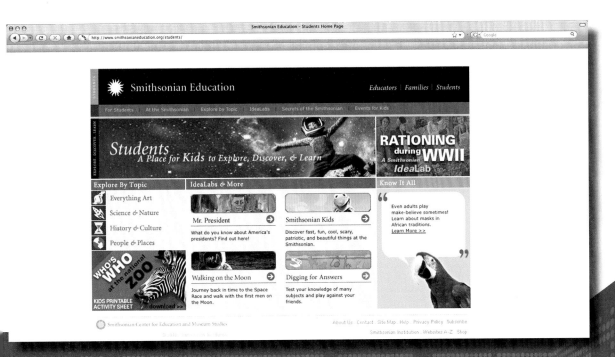

The "Students" section of the Smithsonian Institution's educational Web site (http://www.smithsonianeducation.org) uses well-spaced headings and text blocks arranged in a four-column design. Age-appropriate photographs and illustrations provide visual cues to content, lending the design a kid-friendly feel.

to a GIF or JPEG with an image-processing program. Images must also be sized to fit in the layout and load quickly. If an image is too large, or if the designer doesn't specify its dimensions, the Web browser can take longer to render it on the page.

Above all else, a good Web design is consistent. Banners, backgrounds, colors, fonts, and navigation buttons should have the same appearance from page to page. This way, the visitor can feel comfortable with the design and focus on the content.

Chapter 4

Building a Web Site

nce a Web site has been thoroughly planned and designed, it's time to build it. A good plan will provide a clear road map to follow when it's time to approach the technical side of Web site building. In this phase of development, it's time to consider the appropriate tools for the job, the structure of the HTML code, and the most efficient and intuitive navigation.

Tools for the Job

Web developers build Web sites using software applications called tools. These tools make the job of building the Web site easier and less time consuming. When it comes to building a basic Web site, only a few tools are needed.

The most important tool a Web developer uses is an HTML editor. HTML editors allow people designing Web sites to input HTML code. Many HTML editors also include features that enable people to use dropdown menus to generate the code. With these editors, a user can drag and drop images onto the page, and the editor writes the HTML code that makes

Once the planning stage is completed, Web designers have to sit down and begin the work of actually building the site. Today's Web designers use HTML editors and graphics programs when creating a Web page.

it work on the Internet. One of the big advantages of an HTML editor is that a user can view the code the editor generates. This is a great way to learn how to code HTML. Some hosting sites allow subscribers to use their HTML editors. Popular HTML editors include Adobe CoffeeCup, Dreamweaver, HomeSite, and KompoZer.

Graphics programs are also important tools in Web design. They are used to manipulate images, such as photographs. For example, a graphics program can be used to change the dimensions of an image so it fits on a Web page or to crop images to improve their composition. Popular graphics programs include Adobe Photoshop, Gimp, and PhotoPlus.

Illustration programs enable people to make line drawings and add colors and patterns to a Web site. Some people use illustration programs to make cartoons for their sites or buttons for their navigation menus. Popular illustration tools include Adobe Illustrator, DrawPlus, and Jasc PaintShop Pro.

Building the Home Page
and Secondary Pages

Up to this point, someone building a Web site has a free hand in planning and designing the site. However, during the construction of the site, a few strict rules must be followed. The site must be built using well-formed, valid HTML. This means that the Web site must be coded according to the rules of the World Wide Web Consortium (W3C), which is the governing body that creates Web standards. Code that adheres to these standards will work consistently across various browsers and computer operating systems.

W3C standards require certain elements on each Web page. For instance, each page must begin and end with the <html> tag. Each must have a heading as well. A basic page looks something like this:

```
<html>
<head>
<title>The Title of the Page Goes Here</title>
```

Web design can be a challenging job. Creative individuals who enjoy the hard work required to solve complex problems in an environment of continuously changing technology are drawn to the occupation.

```
</head>
<body>
All text, images, and other elements go here.
</body>
</html>
```

The tags, such as <title> and </title>, surround the content and tell the browser how to display it on the screen. There are many different tags available, and they are used for all sorts of purposes, including changing the size and color of text, putting space between paragraphs, and locating elements on a page.

File   Edit   View   Favorites   Tools   Help

META TAGS

Meta Tags

Web designers use meta tags to create incredibly powerful search capabilities for their Web sites. Meta tags are HTML codes that are inserted into
the header on a Web page, after the title tag. They include information
about the Web site. Specifically, meta tags include the meta description
tag, which is a statement that describes the site, and meta keywords, which
may include any words that appear on or describe the site. Meta tags
do not affect how the page is displayed, and they are not seen by users.
Instead, their main function is to provide meta document data to search
engines. When a potential visitor types a keyword into a search engine, the
search engine looks for the keywords in the meta tags of many thousands of
pages, returning the results that match best.

Today, most Web developers use cascading style sheets (CSS) to
define the way the HTML is displayed on the page. The style sheet is a
separate file containing only tags and instructions for display. Each Web
page refers to this file for display instructions. The advantage of CSS is
that a Web developer can change any style on the Web site just by
editing the style sheet, rather than by editing the HTML of each page of
the site.

Building Navigation Menus

Another important design consideration in the construction of a Web site is
the navigation menu. Navigation menus contain the links a visitor clicks on to
move from one page to another. Because navigation menus are heavily used

Web designers need to keep up with cutting-edge trends and new tools in their field. It is common for them to take tutorials and classes in key specialties like programming, graphic design, and Web site design.

by visitors to a Web site, it's important that special care be taken in their design. They should be user friendly, or even fun to use.

One basic rule is that the navigation menu displays in the same place on every page of the site. Typically, this is horizontally beneath the banner, or vertically on the left side of the page.

On some Web sites, the navigation menu includes links to each page on the site. Other Web sites have navigation menus that link only to the next tier of pages. For example, the navigation menu on the home page links to the tier 2 pages, and the navigation menu on each tier 2 page links to the tier 3 pages.

Navigation menus can be simple or dynamic. A simple navigation menu is simply a list of links. A dynamic navigation menu changes when the visitor runs the cursor over it (this is called "mousing over" something). For example, it may at first appear as a list of only the top-level links. When the visitor mouses over one of the links, a short list of sublinks (also called a drop-down menu) appears. The visitor may then click on one of the sublinks to visit the page. Any number of effects may be added to enhance the user experience. For instance, these can include submenus that fade in or slide down when the mouse hovers over them.

A simple menu is easy to make, loads quickly, and works best for Web sites with no more than sixteen pages. Dropdown navigation menus take up less space on the page and are more fun to use, but they require scripts, such as JavaScript, to build.

MYTHS & FACTS

MYTH The more pages and features on a Web site, the better it is.

FACT More pages and features mean more work for the person building the Web site. Broken links, out-of-date pages, and unused features don't impress anyone. Clear and simple Web sites are generally the most effective. Pages and features can be added as they are needed.

MYTH Once a Web site is built and published, it will immediately be viewed by visitors.

FACT A site can't be visited until someone finds it. Major search engines may not index the site for several months after it is published. Meta tags can be used to draw traffic to a site.

MYTH A person needs to be completely fluent in programming languages before building a Web site.

FACT There are many programs out there that can help anyone design a Web site. Learning a programming language such as CSS can help make a Web site more functional and attractive, but it is not a requirement for Web design.

Chapter 5

Publishing and Maintaining a Web Site

Designing and building the site is only part of the process. Once the Web site is built, it's time to secure a domain and a Web hosting service. A domain is a name for the Web site, and hosting services provide server space where the Web pages can be accessed. Some people have a Web site name in mind when they design a site and will have already shopped around for suitable Web hosts. The site must also be tested thoroughly to make sure each link works and every page loads like it is supposed to.

Acquiring a Domain

Acquiring a domain gives a person the right to use a particular URL for a site. Domain names end with suffixes that denote their purpose: .com and

All of the data associated with a Web site is stored on one or more secure servers. Sometimes the data is stored on many interconnected servers, called server farms.

.net are used for commercial sites; .org is used by nonprofit organizations; and .edu is used by universities.

Domains are generally available through Web hosting services and cost a few dollars a year. The name of the domain usually gives visitors an idea of what kind of Web site they're browsing. An individual may choose any name for his or her Web site's domain, so long as no one else is using it.

Companies that provide Web hosting services use mainstream marketing to attract potential customers and investors. The Web hosting company GoDaddy.com has aired commercials during the Super Bowl and fields a team in the NASCAR Sprint Cup Series.

Getting a Web Host

A Web host is a service where the files that make up a Web site are stored. A Web host owns and manages the Web servers that serve the Web pages to visitors. It rents out server space to people who want to publish Web sites. After subscribing to a Web hosting service, people upload the files that comprise the Web site to the Web host's server when they want to publish the site.

Most Web hosting services are inexpensive, and some are even free. Each has its advantages and disadvantages, and some are better for certain purposes than others. According to tizag.com, there are four types of services:

Minimal shared hosting: Many Web sites share a server. Usually free, this kind of hosting has few features, but it can be great for novice Web designers.

Shared hosting: Many Web sites share a server. Although users must pay a small monthly fee, the service is full featured. Shared hosting is mostly used by individuals and small businesses.

Unmanaged, dedicated server hosting: Used by businesses with server administration expertise, this kind of hosting means that a Web site uses its own server. This enhances security, and the customer conducts all server administration.

Managed, dedicated server hosting: A Web site uses its own server, but the Web hosting service conducts all server administration. This kind of hosting is generally used by businesses that want to leave server administration to the pros.

Going Live: Publishing and Testing

Once the Web site is finished, a tool called a Web validator is used to check for any inconsistencies with W3C standards. The validator looks at the HTML code and shows where any errors appear so they can easily be found and fixed.

File   Edit   View   Favorites   Tools   Help

WIDGETS

Widgets

A widget is a piece of code, called a snippet, that is embedded in the HTML of a Web page. Widgets are created to perform a specific function. For example, there are widgets that display daily weather forecasts, widgets that display slideshows of images, and widgets that can automatically organize blog posts by topic. Web site designers and bloggers use widgets to make their sites more interesting and informative.

After the site has been validated, it is ready to be published to the Web server. This is a matter of uploading the Web site files to the Web hosting service's computer. When the files have been uploaded, the site is "live." Anyone who knows the URL can type it into a browser and request the Web pages.

Once the site is published, it's time for one of the most important tasks: testing. Every page must be checked to make sure it is loading correctly. Every link on every page must also be tested to make sure they work properly. When all of the pages and links check out, the Web site is finished.

Maintenance

Most Web site designers choose to continually update their sites to keep visitors coming back for fresh content. It's a good practice to help visitors find updates to a site. Some Web site designers place the date the new content appeared next to its link or headline. That way, visitors can see exactly when that content was added to the site.

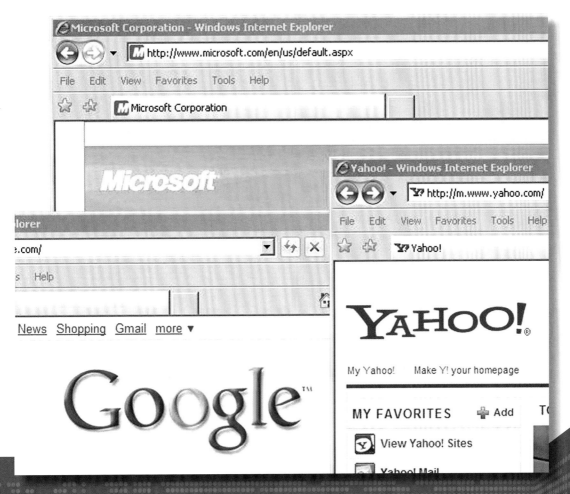

Since the World Wide Web exploded in popularity, computer software giants like Microsoft are finding stiff competition in a market populated by fast-growing start-ups founded on emerging Internet technology.

In addition to updating the Web site, testing is a big part of regular maintenance. Web pages and links should be tested periodically. Most important, the entire site should be retested any time it is updated. At these times, special attention should be paid to links to other Web sites, which sometimes change without notice.

TEN GREAT QUESTIONS

TO ASK A WEB SITE DESIGNER

1. Can I go to college for Web design?

2. How do I get permission to use a particular image on my Web site?

3. How can I determine if I should build a Web site or a blog?

4. What programming or development languages should I learn?

5. How often should I update my Web site or blog?

6. How can I make the pages of my Web site load faster?

7. What kind of HTML editor should I use?

8. How can I track the number of visitors to my site?

9. How do I generate ideas for fresh content?

10. What Web sites and blogs can help me keep up-to-date on Web design trends?

GLOSSARY

cascading style sheets (CSS) A language used to describe the look and formatting of a document written in HTML.

client A workstation on a network that gains access to central data files, programs, and peripheral devices through a server.

code The symbolic arrangement of statements or instructions in a computer program that allow it to operate.

column A division of a page from top to bottom.

data Information that has been translated into a form that can be processed by computers.

document A computer data file or a Web page.

dynamic navigation menu A navigation menu that changes when a visitor mouses over it.

home page The initial page a visitor lands on when he or she navigates to a Web site.

hyperlink An object, such as text or an image, that is linked through hypertext to a Web page.

Internet A network of computers all over the world.

intuitive Referring to direct perception, by sense rather than by reason. In this context, the word describes a navigation system that a visitor may use without having to make conscious decisions.

navigate To move from one page to another on a Web site (or from one Web site to another) using hyperlinks.

network A system containing any combination of computers, printers, audio or visual display devices, or telephones interconnected by telecommunication equipment or cables; used to transmit or receive information.

publish In Web design, publishing is the act of placing a Web site on a Web server and making it available to the public.

security Protection from unauthorized access to a computer or computer network.

site map A diagram that illustrates the structure of a Web site.

tag A keyword or term assigned to a piece of information on a Web page.

target audience The primary group of people that something is aimed at.

tier A layer or level.

Web browser A software application for retrieving and presenting information on the World Wide Web.

Web server A computer program that delivers (or serves) content, such as a Web page.

Computer History Museum
1401 N. Shoreline Boulevard
Mountain View, CA 94043
(650) 810-1010
Web site: http://www.computerhistory.org
This museum has exhibits, events, and activities that focus on the artifacts and
    stories of the information age.

Internet Society
1775 Wiehle Avenue, Suite 201
Reston, VA 20190
(703) 439-2120
Web site: http://www.isoc.org
This organization works to address issues relating to the Internet, including
    Internet education, standards, and policy.

Just Think
39 Mesa Street, Suite 106
San Francisco, CA 94129
(415) 561-2900
Web site: http://justthink.org
This foundation is dedicated to helping young people build their critical
    thinking and creative media production skills.

Media Awareness Network
1500 Merivale Road, 3rd Floor
Ottawa, ON K2E 6Z5
Canada
(613) 224-7721

Web site: http://www.media-awareness.ca
The Media Awareness Network is dedicated to promoting digital and
    media literacy.

World Wide Web Consortium (W3C)
77 Massachusetts Avenue
MIT Room 32-G524
Cambridge, MA 02139
Web site: http://www.w3.org
The World Wide Web Consortium (W3C) is an international community
    where organizations, a full-time staff, and the public work together to
    develop Web standards.

Web Sites

Due to the changing nature of Internet links, Rosen Publishing has developed
an online list of Web sites related to the subject of this book. This site is
updated regularly. Please use this link to access the list:

http://www.rosenlinks.com/dil/site

FOR FURTHER READING

Chapman, Nigel, and Jenny Chapman. *Web Design: A Complete Introduction*. Hoboken, NJ: Wiley, 2007.

Derfler, Frank, and Les Freed. *How Networks Work*. Indianapolis, IN: Que, 2004.

Farrell, Mary. *Computer Programming for Teens*. Boston, MA: Course Technology PTR, 2007.

Frey, Tara. *Blogging for Bliss: Crafting Your Own Online Journal: A Guide for Crafters, Artists, and Creatives of All Kinds*. New York, NY: Lark Books, 2009.

Gardner, Susannah, and Shane Birley. *Blogging for Dummies*. Hoboken, NJ: Wiley, 2008.

Gralla, Preston. *How the Internet Works*. Indianapolis, IN: Que, 2006.

Gralla, Preston. *Online Activities for Kids: Projects for School, Extra Credit, or Just Plain Fun*. New York, NY: Wiley, 2001.

Jenkins, Sue. *Web Design for Dummies*. Indianapolis, IN: For Dummies, 2009.

Jenkins, Sue. *Web Design: The L Line, the Express Line to Learning*. Hoboken, NJ: Wiley, 2007.

Johnson, Jeff. *Web Bloopers: 60 Common Web Design Mistakes and How to Avoid Them*. San Francisco, CA: Morgan Kaufman, 2003.

Miller, Michael. *Absolute Beginner's Guide to Computer Basics*. Indianapolis, IN: Que, 2009.

Millhollon, Mary, Jeff Castrina, and Leslie Lothamer. *Easy Web Design*. Redmond, WA: Microsoft Press, 2006.

Quick, Richard. *Web Design in Easy Steps*. Warwickshire, England: In Easy Steps Limited, 2007.

Robbins, Jennifer Niederst. *Learning Web Design: A Beginner's Guide to Learning HTML, CSS, Graphics, and Beyond*. Sebastopol, CA: O'Reilly Media, 2007.

Sabin-Wilson, Lisa. *WordPress for Dummies*. Hoboken, NJ: Wiley, 2009.

Sande, Warren, and Carter Sande. *Hello World!: Computer Programming for Kids and Other Beginners*. Greenwich, CT: Manning Publications, 2009.

Sethi, Maneesh. *Game Programming for Teens*. Boston, MA: Course Technology PTR, 2008.

Smith, Jim. *How to Start a Home-Based Web Design Business*. 3rd ed. Guilford, CT: Globe Pequot, 2007.

White, Ron, and Timothy Edward Downs. *How Computers Work*. Indianapolis, IN: Que, 2007.

BIBLIOGRAPHY

Brain, Marshall. "How Web Servers Work." How Stuff Works. Retrieved
September 17, 2009 (http://computer.howstuffworks.com/
Web -server1.htm).

Build Web Site for You. "Web Site Structure." Retrieved October 21, 2009
(http://www.buildwebsite4u.com/building/structure.shtml).

Chapman, Nigel, and Jenny Chapman. Web Design: A Complete
Introduction. Hoboken, NJ: Wiley, 2007.

Connolly, Dan. "A Little History of the World Wide Web." W3C. Retrieved
October 6, 2009 (http://www.w3.org/History.html).

Cooper, Charles. "Web 2.0: Obsolete Within Three Years?" CNET
News, April 23, 2008. Retrieved October 6, 2009 (http://news.
cnet.com/8301-10787_3-9927521-60.html).

Cyberjournalist.net. "How Many Blogs Are There? 50 Million and Counting."
August 7, 2006. Retrieved February 28, 2010 (http://www.
cyberjournalist.net/how-many-blogs-are-there-50-million-and-counting).

Google.com. "Google Analytics IQ Lessons." Retrieved
November 9, 2009 (http://www.google.com/support/
conversionuniversity/?hl=en).

Holden, Greg. Creating Web Pages for Kids and Parents. Foster City, CA:
IDG Books Worldwide, 1997.

Internet Society. "Histories of the Internet." Retrieved September 28, 2009
(http://www.isoc.org/Internet/history).

Irby, Lisa. "How to Plan a Website." 2 Plan a Website. Retrieved October 8,
2009 (http://www.2planawebsite.com).

Lissa Explains It All. "Basics." Retrieved October 6, 2009 (http://www.
lissaexplains.com/basics.shtml).

Lissa Explains It All. "CSS." Retrieved November 9, 2009 (http://www.
lissaexplains.com/css.shtml).

Lissa Explains It All. "Tools." Retrieved October 23, 2009 (http://www.
    lissaexplains.com/tools.shtml).

Lynch, Patrick J., and Sarah Horton. *Web Style Guide: Basic Design
    Principles for Creating Web Sites*. New Haven, CT: Yale University
    Press, 2008.

Olsen, Eric. "Dan Gillmore Interview: SOTB 2009." Technorati.com,
    October 22, 2009. Retrieved November 9, 2009 (http://
    technorati.com/blogging/article/dan-gillmor-interview-sotb-2009).

Sethi, Maneesh. *Web Design for Teens*. Boston, MA: Thomson Course
    Technology PTR, 2005.

Tizag.com. "Web Host Types." Retrieved October 6, 2009 (http://www.
    tizag.com/webhost/host_types.php).

Watrall, Ethan, and Siarto, Jeff. *Head First Web Design*. Sebastopol, CA:
    O'Reilly Media, 2008.

W3schools.com. "What Is the WWW?" Retrieved October 6, 2009
    (http://www.w3schools.com/Web /Web _www.asp).

INDEX

About the Author

As a technical writer and editor, J. Poolos has been helping people of all ages use computer software for eighteen years. He has designed and developed Web sites professionally, and he has authored more than fifteen books for young adults.

Photo Credits

Cover (left), p. 1 (left), p. 27 © www.istockphoto.com/Marina Bartel; cover (second from left, right), p. 1 (second from left, right), p. 11 © www.istockphoto.com; cover (second from right), p. 1 (second from right), p. 33 © www.istockphoto.com/Amy Walters; cover (background), interior design © www.istockphoto.com; p. 7 Issouf Sanogo/AFP/Getty Images; p. 10 © www.istockphoto.com/Chris Schmidt; p. 16 © AP Images; p. 25 © www.istockphoto.com/Alexandra Draghici; p. 29 Shutterstock; p. 34 Jerry Mackland/Getty Images for NASCAR; p. 37 Bloomberg/Bloomberg via Getty Images.

Designer: Nicole Russo; Photo Researcher: Marty Levick